101 READING Activities

Contributing Writers
Suzanne I. Barchers, Ed.D.
Marilee Robin Burton
Beth Alley Wise

Consultant
Leslie Anne Perry, Ph.D.

Illustrators
Kate Flanagan
Lynn Sweat

pil

Publications International, Ltd.

D0731144

Contributing Writers

Suzanne I. Barchers, Ed.D., has written numerous books and articles on reading, language arts, and literacy for children. She serves as an affiliate faculty member at the University of Colorado, Denver, and is a former educator, reading specialist, and administrator at public and private schools in Denver.

Marilee Robin Burton is a freelance educational writer, consultant, and language arts specialist. She has ten years of experience as a teacher and has contributed to several publications, including *Early Childhood Workshop* and *Literary Place.* She is also the author and artist for several children's picture books and has a master of arts degree in early childhood education and human development.

Beth Alley Wise is an early childhood education specialist and the author of more than 50 children's books, including *Beginning to Read, Key Words to Reading,* and *My Reading Kit.* She has written and edited textbooks and software for numerous educational publishers and serves as a developmental specialist on reading reforms.

Consultant

Leslie Anne Perry, Ph.D., is Assistant Professor for the Department of Curriculum and Instruction at East Tennessee State University. She has a Ph.D. in elementary education with a specialization in reading and a masters of science degree in early childhood education. She has contributed to instructional books on reading for educators, and her articles have appeared in several educational publications, including *Educational Oasis, Teaching K–8,* and *Illinois Reading Council Journal.*

Additional consultation was provided by Elizabeth Crosby Stull, Ph.D., Assistant Professor of Language and Literacy, Childrens' Literature, The Ohio State University. She has written several books, including curriculum activity guides for The Center for Applied Research in Education, and is a member of the International Reading Association and the National Association for Education of Young Children.

Illustrators: Kate Flanagan, Lynn Sweat
Front and Back Cover Illustrations: Anne Kennedy

Louis Weber, CEO
Publications International, Ltd.
7373 North Cicero Avenue
Lincolnwood, Illinois 60712

Permission is never granted for commercial purposes.

ISBN-13: 978-1-4127-1369-6

ISBN-10: 1-4127-1369-2

Manufactured in China.

8 7 6 5 4 3 2 1

Contents

MAKE READING FUN!

101 Reading Activities contains an appealing array of exciting, motivating, and educational language arts activities, all of which contribute to your child's reading development.

Reading, writing, listening, and speaking are the four major areas of language arts. Each of these language forms reinforces the other. Therefore, activities that focus on writing,

listening, and speaking develop and reinforce skills necessary for reading success. From creating picture dictionaries and word webs to inventive storytelling and creative writing, your child will gain a better understanding of the elements needed to become a more confident reader.

When guiding your child through these activities, your goal should always be to provide a positive learning experience. Take the time to go over the instructions carefully with your child, have patience, and use praise and encouragement. Each activity has been rated with a difficulty level: *easy, medium,* or *challenging.* Book symbols near the title of each activity represent the degree of difficulty: Three books indicate activities that are challenging, two books indicate activities that require intermediate skills, and one book indicates activities that are easy. And even though the activities are labeled by their level of difficulty, *all* activities are on the same level of fun. These designations are here to provide guidance as you select activities for your child. Remember, though, that children learn at

activities designed to enhance a particular skill. The first four chapters relate specifically to reading, followed by three chapters related to writing, two chapters that cover listening and speaking, and one chapter that focuses on developing thinking skills.

Chapter 1 (Literature Links) is designed to get the child started on a lifetime of pleasure with books. Through the activities in this chapter, your child will develop the habit of reading. After all, reading is the key that opens the door to a whole world of information.

Reading without comprehension or understanding, however, is not actual reading. Chapter 2 (Comprehension Capers) offers an exciting array of activities designed to generate enthusiasm for reading while building skills necessary for comprehension.

different rates. An activity that may be easy for one child may be challenging for another child of the same age. Therefore, regardless of the age of your child, you may want to start with some of the activities designated as *easy* and work up. All of the activities in this book can be enhanced through interaction with an adult. However, some of the activities require close adult supervision for safety reasons, such as activities that require the use of scissors or other implements; some even involve cooking. Be sure to read all the instructions carefully and adhere to any words of caution.

This book is divided into ten chapters. Each chapter focuses on a different element of reading and contains a wide variety of

Written passages that a child reads are made up of individual words. Your child can read with comprehension only if they recognize and understand the meaning of these words. The activities in Chapter 3 (Word Quests) engage your child in lively wordplay while improving basic vocabulary skills.

Chapter 4 (Phonics Fortunes) delves into reinforcing word recognition skills, which allow the child to read more independently. Creative activities such as Letter Collages and Simon Says offer inventive and fun ways for the child to learn letter sounds. And learning to apply phonics skills to unknown words will help the child comprehend what is being read.

Chapter 5 (Writing Roundups), the first of the writing chapters, presents

activities that strengthen and reinforce reading skills through poems, songs, and other writing exercises. Reading and writing are simply two heads of the same coin. The child who is a competent writer usually excels at reading, and vice versa.

Spelling is one of the tools that makes written communication possible. Chapter 6 (Spelling Specials) offers an inventive selection of spelling escapades to reinforce your child's spelling skills. Spelling and phonics are closely related. The child who learns to attend to the sounds represented by letters while learning to spell words can use this knowledge of letter/sound relationships when he or she decodes unknown words encountered while reading.

Grammar is another tool that enhances written communication. Chapter 7 (Grammar

Grabbers) focuses on appealing activities that help the young reader develop knowledge about parts of speech and other elements of grammar, such as the use of nouns, verbs, and adjectives.

Listening is the first communication skill children utilize. Chapter 8 (Listening Launches) invites the young learner to enhance good listening skills through this selection of fun listening activities.

Speaking, an integral part of oral language development, is also closely related to reading development. Chapter 9 (Speaking Sparks) introduces activities that help develop speaking skills, for it is much easier for the child to learn to read words already used verbally.

The final chapter, Chapter 10 (Using Brainpower), helps develop the child's thinking skills. Cognitive processing (thinking) is central to all four of the language arts, and the development of critical thinking skills is essential for reading success.

JOAN STEALS HOME!

The activities within the various chapters are not in any particular order, so feel free to skip around throughout the book. Your child may respond well to a particular type of activity. For example, if your child likes to look at pictures in magazines, you may want to follow up on another day with a picture activity. The new activity could be from the same chapter or from a different chapter. In order to keep track of the activities you and your child have done, you may want to use a pencil to make a check mark beside each activity as it is completed.

It is the sincere hope of the authors and editors of *101 Reading Activities* that the ideas presented in this book will be helpful to you as you work with your child during these very special years. You play a critical role in your child's reading development—you are your child's first teacher. With your guidance, your child can grow in both competence and confidence as he or she embarks on one of life's most wondrous and rewarding adventures—reading!

LITERATURE LINKS

Children who are read to at home actually do better in reading at school. In addition, the child is exposed to new vocabulary words and how they sound. The child also gains familiarity with books and learns that print is read from left to right. The following activities in this chapter range from dressing up as a favorite character to eating through the alphabet. Some require a trip to the library; others require only a trip to your bookshelf. Many of the books will inspire you to create your own reading activities.

ALPHABET EATING

The child will learn new food words while creating a menu for many meals to come.

WHAT YOU'LL NEED: alphabet book that deals with food

Read the alphabet book together. Then read the book again, but this time have the child point to and read the words. Next list all the foods illustrated and organize them from *A* to *Z*. Some letters will have more than one food, other letters will have none, but include all of them.

Now plan what foods to eat over the course of a week, with the intention of eating through the alphabet. Use the letters with several choices to provide a series of menus that are balanced and interesting. Write up a menu for each meal, and have the child read the food words. At the end of the week evaluate the process. Was it fun? Did the child learn some new words and try some new foods?

2

CLIFF-HANGERS

The child will enjoy reading a good cliff-hanger while practicing reading and comprehension skills.

WHAT YOU'LL NEED: *Charlotte's Web* or *The Trumpet of the Swan* by E. B. White, tape recorder

Read one of the above "cliff-hanger" stories into a tape recorder. Then have the child read the book while listening to the tape. This will help the child read and understand the text. After each chapter, stop the tape recorder and invite the child to predict what will happen next. Discuss the prediction together. Then have the child read the next chapter to find out if the prediction is correct. Continue the activity until the book is finished.

CREATING A CHARACTER

3

An imaginative child will enjoy becoming a favorite character for a day!

WHAT YOU'LL NEED: favorite book or story, dress-up clothes

Invite the child to choose a character from a favorite book. Help the child find descriptive passages that tell about the character. Then invite the child to decide how the character would dress and act. For example, the child can put on a red cape and carry a basket of goodies. Have a dress-up day when the child dresses up as the character and reads portions of the book aloud.

4 MATCH THAT PICTURE!

In this activity, the beginning reader will practice comprehension while matching words with pictures.

WHAT YOU'LL NEED: any picture book that features many illustrations of objects

Before reading the book aloud, look at all the illustrations and discuss them with the child. Invite the child to point to and name interesting objects in the illustrations. Then read the story aloud to the child while he or she looks on. Have the child find words in the text that match the objects in the illustrations. If there are illustrations without matching words, list the words on a piece of paper and discuss their meanings.

ACTIVITY TWIST

To encourage creative thinking, read a story with no pictures. Then help the child determine what illustrations might be used in the story.

NEW ENDINGS

5

▼▼▼▼▼▼▼▼▼▼▼▼▼▼▼▼▼▼▼▼▼▼▼▼▼▼▼▼▼▼▼▼

*The child will learn how to write new story endings
after reading this popular book.*

WHAT YOU'LL NEED: *Jumanji* by Chris Van Allsburg, paper, pencil

In this book, Peter and Judy find a game called "Jumanji, A Jungle Adventure Game." While playing the game, it comes to life and they must carefully follow the rules to escape life-threatening situations. When Peter and Judy are finished, they return the game to a park where the Budwing children, known for never following instructions, pick up the game.

Begin by reading the book together. Discuss what might happen if the Budwing children play the game by not following the rules. Then write the Budwing's story together to share with others.

SPORTS HEROES

6

▬▬ ▬▬ ▬▬ ▬▬ ▬▬ ▬▬ ▬▬ ▬▬ ▬▬ ▬▬ ▬▬ ▬▬

*This creative reading and recording activity
is for sports fans of all ages.*

WHAT YOU'LL NEED: book about a favorite sports figure, newspapers or magazines with information about the person, notebook, pencil

Read through a book about a favorite sports figure together. Then scan the newspapers or magazines for additional information about the person. Invite the child to start a notebook that records facts or statistics about the sports figure. Add to it regularly.

THE MORAL OF THE STORY

7

What better way to teach a lesson than through a little story?

WHAT YOU'LL NEED: collection of fables

Fables are short stories, usually involving animals, that teach lessons. Many are attributed to Aesop, the famous Greek writer of fables. Find one or more fables, and take turns reading them. How many have people in them? Animals? What is the most common animal? For an additional challenge, make a list that keeps track of the number of foxes, crows, and other animals found in the fables. Then discuss what lessons are to be learned from each story.

CREEPY CRAWLIES

8

Using an interest in insects is a great way to inspire children to read information books.

WHAT YOU'LL NEED: any information book with photographs or drawings of spiders, ants, or other insects; notebook; pencil

Information books often have bright, colorful pictures, charts, and boxes containing special information. Together, choose a particular creepy crawly, such as the ant, that is found in the book. Invite the child to read everything in the book about ants. Then look for ants outside together. Have the child make notes about the ants and compare the notes to the information found in the book. This process can be repeated several times during different seasons to see the changes that occur in the behavior of the chosen creepy crawly.

COMPREHENSION CAPERS

Comprehension is about understanding ideas through sentences. The activities contained in this chapter are designed to help the child develop into a confident reader who comprehends what is being read. The child will explore the main idea and supporting details while giggling through Opening a Can of Worms, get a real taste of sequencing in Flip, Flap, Flop, and sharpen their skills at story comprehension in Step-by-Step. Additional activities are sure to generate enthusiasm for reading while building skills necessary for comprehension.

STACK-A-STORY

·   9

Busy hands will love the challenge of this story-building activity.

WHAT YOU'LL NEED: 3-6 cardboard boxes, poster paints, paintbrushes

Set out boxes and materials for painting. Discuss the main events in a story you and the child have recently read together. Then assist the child in painting a story scene on each cardboard box. When the boxes are dry, have the child stack them in rows so they can be read from left to right. Invite the child to retell the story in sequential order.

OPENING A CAN OF WORMS

The child will wiggle and giggle while learning about main ideas and supporting details.

WHAT YOU'LL NEED: tin can, construction paper, clear tape, felt-tip pens, precut worms made from construction paper or poster board, familiar story

Begin by wrapping a tin can with construction paper and securing it with tape. Write the main idea of a familiar story on the outside of the tin can, turning the can around so the child will not see it. On each precut worm, write a supporting detail to the story, then place all the worms in the can. Explain that supporting details are pieces of information that work together to help tell the main idea. You may also want to discuss how each story has a beginning, middle, and end. Invite the child to pick worms from the can and read the sentences written on them. From this, have the child identify the main idea of the story.

GREETING CARDS

Build an understanding of an author's purpose, audience, and main idea by creating a friendly greeting.

WHAT YOU'LL NEED: construction paper, clear tape or glue, blunt scissors, art and craft scraps, felt-tip pens, envelopes, postage stamps

Discuss a list of greetings together, such as hello, get well, congratulations, happy birthday, and I love you. Invite the child to write a greeting on a piece of construction paper, and decorate it with art scraps. Then have the child explain whom the card is for (the audience), why it was made (author's purpose), and what greeting was written (main idea). You may want to assist the child with addressing and stamping the envelopes to mail.

REPORT CARDS

12

Make a mock report card to see if characters in favorite stories and books make the grade.

WHAT YOU'LL NEED: construction paper, felt-tip pen

On a folded piece of construction paper, invite the child to make a report card with at least three areas for grading a story character. Include some of the following: helpfulness, attitude, sense of humor, completing assignments, following rules, and being on time. The report is not complete until the child "grades" the character in each of the selected areas. The child may even find it necessary to request a conference with the character's parents. If so, this should be noted on the report card, too.

13

FUNNY DAYS

The calendar will never be the same with this fun, day-renaming activity.

WHAT YOU'LL NEED: calendar, poster board, markers

Before beginning this activity, look at a calendar together and point out the following to the child: the month and year, days of the week, numbers for the days, and special events. After setting out poster board and markers, invite the child to design a calendar for one week, like the example shown here. Have the child create new names for the days of the week based on his or her scheduled activities or how he or she feels about a particular day. For example, the child may rename Saturday *Soccerday* and rename Friday *Funday.*

NEWS OF THE DAY!

Explore main ideas as the child writes headlines for a day's events and activities.

WHAT YOU'LL NEED: newspaper, magnetic letters, magnetic surface or refrigerator door

Recall the events the child was involved in on a particular day. Discuss the most important and the most memorable events. Which event or events would other people want to know about?

Page through a newspaper together. Point out the headlines to the child. Explain that a headline is used to provide a glimpse of what's in the article and entice the reader to read the article.

Display uppercase and lowercase magnetic letters on a magnetic surface. Let the child manipulate the letters freely for a few minutes, then invite the child to arrange the letters to create a headline describing a highlight of the day.

ACTIVITY TWIST

For an additional challenge, point to a particular headline in the newspaper and ask the child to guess what the story is about. See how accurate the child and the headline are.

THEME DOMINOES

15

*This version of dominoes is a matching activity
based on the popular children's game.*

WHAT YOU'LL NEED: poster board, old magazines, blunt scissors, clear tape or glue

Decide on a category, such as furniture, animals, or transportation, and make dominoes that depict several objects in the chosen category. (The pictures don't need to be identical, but the categories should be clear to the child.) The dominoes can be made by cutting and taping or gluing small pictures from old magazines on precut poster board rectangles. Explain to the child that pictures of each object should appear on at least three dominoes. Then play dominoes using the following rules of the traditional game.

Turn dominoes facedown on a table. Each player picks five dominoes and places the pieces faceup in front of them. Players then take turns placing one domino at a time on the board. A domino may only be placed on the board if one of its halves matches a domino already on the board. For

example, if the domino on the board has a picture of a moving van, a player can only place a matching domino on the board. Matching dominoes can be placed end to end or end to side. If a player does not have a match, he or she must pick from the remaining dominoes until a match is found. The first player to run out of dominoes is the winner.

FLIP, FLAP, FLOP

16

*The child will flip while uncovering
directions in sequence!*

WHAT YOU'LL NEED: 12×18-inch piece of paper folded in
half lengthwise, blunt scissors, crayons or markers

Invite the child to describe steps in a familiar process,
such as preparing a bowl of cereal, building a wooden block
castle, or brushing teeth. Help the child cut three or more flaps in
the paper, depending on the number of steps in the process. (There
should be one flap for each step.) Cut from the edge of the paper toward
the fold. Then have the child write the steps on the underside of the sheet, one
step underneath each flap. Then write the corresponding numeral (1, 2, 3) to show
the order of the steps on the covering flap. Have the child turn up each flap as he
or she describes the sequence.

17

STEP-BY-STEP

*While learning how to formulate questions, the child
will enhance story comprehension.*

Begin by having one player take on the role of a character from a favorite story both players have
read. Next have the other player try to guess the identity of the character by asking a maximum of
ten questions that can be answered "yes" or "no." For example, suggest the following: Are you a
person? Are you an animal? Do you have fur? Did you ever blow down a straw house?

Take turns with different characters, and see how many questions it takes to guess the character.
The player who correctly identifies the character using the least amount of questions is the winner.

PRONOUN BINGO

18

The child will have fun playing this familiar game of wits and luck while learning about pronouns.

WHAT YOU'LL NEED: cardboard, felt-tip pens, game markers (beans, paper squares, bottle caps)

B	I	N	G	O
HE	SHE	THEY	IT	WE
ME				

Make cardboard bingo game boards, and write a pronoun in each square. (Pronouns include *he, she, we, they, it, I, me, her, him, us, them, mine, yours, hers, his, its, ours, theirs.*) You will repeat some pronouns, but the child can choose which pronoun to cover. Make sure every board is different. To play, call out names of people, objects, or animals, both singular and plural, and have players cover the square with any pronoun that applies to the name called. The first player to cover five squares in a row is the winner.

19

FINGER PAINT FOLLIES

These tasty replacements for finger paint provide an easy-to-cleanup and fun-to-use method to paint predictions.

WHAT YOU'LL NEED: smock, whipped cream or ready-made pudding, sponges, pail of water, unfamiliar nursery rhyme

Have the child put on an old smock. Invite the child to spread whipped cream or pudding on the top of a clean kitchen table, preferably one with a surface that can be easily cleaned with sponges and water. Then read a nursery rhyme that is unfamiliar to the child. At some point in the rhyme, pause and ask the child to finger-paint a picture to show what he or she predicts will happen next.

Repeat this activity with other nursery rhymes. Have the child "erase" the previous drawing by rubbing over it with his or her hands. The child can then sponge the excess pudding or whipped cream off the table when finished.

RAIN DANCE

*Defining main ideas becomes a lively performance
when a little song and dance is done.*

Sing the song "Eensy Weensy Spider" together. Discuss the main idea of the song. Then work with the child to create a dance showing the spider going up and down the waterspout. Have the child perform the dance while the song is being played or sung. Repeat this activity using other familiar songs such as "Frosty the Snowman," "I'm a Little Teapot," and "Oh Where, Oh Where Has My Little Dog Gone?"

For added fun, invite other children to add details to the song by dancing or pantomiming the parts of the sun shining, the rain falling, flowers opening, and so on.

WORD QUESTS

Children are naturally curious about their environment. They use their keen eyes and developing senses of taste, smell, touch, and hearing to explore the world around them. The language they hear associated with their experiences forms the foundation for their listening, speaking, reading, and writing vocabularies. In this chapter, vocabulary instruction comes alive for children, motivating even the most reluctant learners through engaging games and activities. Whether the child plays Tic-Tac-Toe a Word, is amused with Bubblegum Words, or just gets tickled with Compound Caterpillars, you can be sure he or she will have fun while improving basic vocabulary skills.

ABC ACTION

21

A, B, C, D, E, F, Gee, it's fun to pantomime action words with this up-and-at-'em action activity.

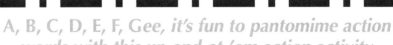

WHAT YOU'LL NEED: paper, pencil, construction paper, crayons or markers

What do the words *run, skip, climb, eat, plant, fly,* and *sing* have in common? They are action words, or verbs. Make a list of action words together, then ask the child to choose a word from the list to pantomime. Invite the child to illustrate the action by writing the word on a piece of paper, making the first letter perform the action. For example, a child may write the word *sing* in which the *s* is singing, or write the word *run* in which the *r* appears to be running.

STICKUPS

●●●●●●●●●●●●●●●●●●●●●●●●●●●●●●●●●●●

22

Forming words from mixed-up letters is an exciting and educational way for the child to learn story vocabulary.

WHAT YOU'LL NEED: magnetic letters, magnetic surface, favorite book or story

Select an interesting word from a favorite book or story, and collect magnetic letters to make that word. Use a safe working surface to display the letters, such as a magnetic board, a refrigerator door, the front of a washing machine, or a metal file cabinet. Then scramble the letters. Next invite the child to unscramble the letters to create the known word. You may want to provide clues to help the child guess the word. Continue the activity with more words from the story.

23

TIC-TAC-TOE A WORD

Try this new twist on the popular children's game.

WHAT YOU'LL NEED: paper, ruler, felt-tip pens, 2 colors of sticky notes

Make two tic-tac-toe boards, one for each player, by drawing three rows of three squares on a piece of paper. The squares should be relatively large, at least 1½×1½ inches. Next the players should decide on nine words, perhaps theme-related words (such as foods, animals, favorite story characters) or recently learned vocabulary words, and write them in random order in the squares on each of the tic-tac-toe boards.

The game is played as in regular tic-tac-toe, except that each player must say the word and use it in a sentence before it can be covered with a sticky note. The first player to cover three words in a row—either across, down, or diagonally—wins the game.

PREFIX SLIP

Create a bevy of different words with this charming approach to prefixes.

WHAT YOU'LL NEED: 5×8-inch rectangle of heavy paper or poster board, ruler, 12×3-inch strip of heavy paper or poster board, blunt scissors, markers

Help the child cut two horizontal slits in the rectangle of poster board, just above and below the center and to the right. The slits should be about four inches long and two inches apart. Then have the child write a prefix in the space to the left of the slits as shown. Common prefixes include but are not limited to: *un, re, dis, pre, de,* and *ex.* Then help the child write on the strip a list of words that can be added to the prefix to form a new word. Explain that by pulling the strip through the slits, the child can make and read new words with the designated prefix.

BUBBLEGUM WORDS

25

Every dentist will like these absolutely cavity-free bubblegum activities!

What happens when you take one end of the bubblegum you are chewing and pull on it? It stretches! The same thing can happen to words. Words can get longer when extra letters are added to the beginning or the end. Write the word *and,* and show how to stretch it to make the words *hand* and *handcuff.* Then invite the child to stretch their own words from *and.* Use a children's dictionary if necessary.

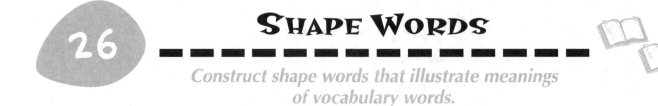

SHAPE WORDS

Construct shape words that illustrate meanings of vocabulary words.

WHAT YOU'LL NEED: markers or crayons, paper

Have the child choose vocabulary words that name objects, insects, or animals. Encourage creative thinking as the child writes the words so that the letters conform to the shape of the object. For example, the letters c-a-t-e-r-p-i-l-l-a-r may be written to take on the curved shape of the insect, as in the example shown, or the letters k-i-t-e may be written with tall letters to fit the diamond-shape object.

ACTIVITY TWIST

The interested child can take the project a step further and create a concrete poem. Explain that concrete poetry is when words in a poem are arranged to make a picture of what the poem is about.

CATEGORY CHALLENGE

You'll need to sharpen your pencil and your wits for this word category game.

WHAT YOU'LL NEED: paper, pencil

Have the child draw a grid on a piece of paper, six squares across and four squares down. Next choose four consonants and one vowel, and write them in boxes two through six across the top. Think of categories, and list them down the left side. Then invite the child to try to complete the game board within a designated time period (3–10 minutes). The object is to come up with a word that begins with each letter in the top row and is part of the category listed.

	B	G	S	R	A
ANIMAL	bear	goat	snake	rat	ape
FOOD	banana		soup	radish	apple

28 JINGLE, JANGLE

*Children will love this action-packed verb game,
and it will strengthen their imagination.*

Have the child write the first letter of his or her name. Then invite the child to write as many *verbs,* or action words, as he or she can think of that begin with the same letter. As a follow-up to the activity, see how many *nouns*—names of people, places, or things—the child can list.

COMPOUND CATERPILLARS 29

*The child will enjoy this interesting take on compound
words while making construction paper caterpillars.*

WHAT YOU'LL NEED: 11×4-inch construction paper caterpillar cutouts, markers or crayons

Explain to the child that a compound word is two separate words that are combined to make one word. Take turns naming compound words. Write the words on a chart. Then set out precut paper caterpillars, similar to those shown here. The child can then fold the left and right ends of the caterpillar cutouts in to meet at the middle. Have the child write words on the outside flaps of the cutout—one word for each flap—that make up a particular compound word from the chart. Next have the child unfold the flaps and write the compound word on the inside of the caterpillar. Invite the child to share the finished work with others.

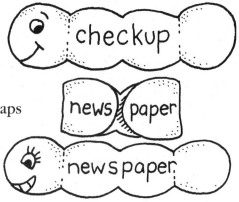

SIMPLE AS A SIMILE

30

Though it's neither as tall as a skyscraper or as strong as an ox, this simile activity is sure to be a big, big hit.

WHAT YOU'LL NEED: bag, several small household objects, poetry collection

Have the child read poems that use *similes.* Point out the similes, and explain that these phrases use the words *as* or *like* to compare two things. Next place several small objects in a bag. Let the child remove one object at a time from the bag and use a simile to describe or compare its size to another object. Use the following format to get the child thinking:

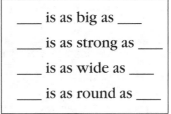

____ is as big as ____

____ is as strong as ____

____ is as wide as ____

____ is as round as ____

PHONICS FORTUNES

In this imaginative array of phonics activities, the child will learn, review, and practice basic phonics skills such as initial consonant sounds, short and long vowel sounds, prefixes and suffixes, *r*-controlled vowels, and much, much more. Whether playing Simon Says, making a Phonics Salad, or creating a Star Mobile, the child will be sure to have fun with phonics!

31 LETTER COLLAGES

Cut it, glue it, paste it! This creative activity is sure to keep busy hands interested in phonics.

WHAT YOU'LL NEED: ABC books, heavy paper (precut into large letters), old magazines, blunt scissors, clear tape or glue, hole punch, string

Read aloud a variety of ABC books with the child. Point out the pictures, the letters, and the corresponding beginning sounds as you read. Next give the child large paper letters that you have cut out in advance. Ask the child to cut out pictures from old magazines of objects that begin with the sound each letter stands for—for example, a cat and car for the letter *C,* and a dog, deer, and door for the letter *D.* Encourage the child to cover the entire letter with the pictures to create a colorful letter collage. To complete the project, punch a hole in the top of each letter and hang it in a room.

32

DEAR WISE OWL

*Invite the child to solve this mini-mystery
about a surprise box.*

WHAT YOU'LL NEED: large piece of construction paper, markers, notebook paper, pencil

Read the following letter to the child:

Dear Wise Owl,

When I opened the front door this morning, there was a large box on my doorstep. It was wrapped in shiny red paper and had a giant bow. Just as I was about to open the box, it moved! What do you think is in the box? What should I do with it?

Please tell me what you think!

Brandon

Have the child write the letters of the alphabet down the left side of a large piece of construction paper. Ask him or her to suggest creative ideas for what may be in the box. Invite the child to think of a word that begins with each letter or as many of the letters as he or she can, and write them on a sheet of paper. Have the child decide on one item from the list that he or she thinks is most likely in the box. Then help the child write a response to Brandon, telling him what the child thinks is in the box and what he or she thinks Brandon should do about it.

SPORTSWRITERS

33

In every sporting event, sportwriters need to be there to get the story. So grab your pencil!

WHAT YOU'LL NEED: old newspapers, blunt scissors, pencils, newspaper, clear tape or glue

Invite the child to pretend to be a sportswriter. Page through the sports section of a newspaper to familiarize the child with headlines, photo captions, and stories. Then help the child collect the tools for the next assignment, including a pencil or two, paper, and some newspapers. Explain that his or her task is to capture, in a single sentence, the main idea or most important moment of a sporting event. Explain how important this story is and how it will appear on the front page of tomorrow's sports section in the local newspaper.

First have the young sportswriter cut out a picture of someone participating in a sport. Invite the child to write a caption or headline, such as the one pictured here, about the athlete using as many words as possible with a particular phonics sound, such as long *o*. Glue or tape the headline and the picture on newsprint to resemble a newspaper.

34

SIMON SAYS

Simon says that children and adults alike will love this silly version of the popular game.

Remind players of the rules for Simon Says. Explain that you will play the game as it is normally played, with the following exception: The players should only follow a command if it begins with a *w* (or another target letter). For example, players can walk, wave, waddle, and wiggle but never hop, clap, or sing.

35 CORNER-TO-CORNER PUZZLE

This twist on the crossword puzzle helps the child practice words containing r-controlled vowels.

WHAT YOU'LL NEED: paper, pencil

Draw a corner-to-corner puzzle on paper like the one shown here. Explain the following phonics rule pertaining to vowels followed by *r: ar* stands for the sound you hear in *star; or* stands for the sound you hear in *horse; ir, ur,* and *er* stand for the sounds you hear in *skirt, nurse,* and *fern.* After reviewing the sounds, give picture or word clues for each *r*-controlled vowel and let the child point out the correct word. As the child masters the sounds, don't write in the *ar, or, ir, ur* or *er* sounds. Let the child write those in him- or herself.

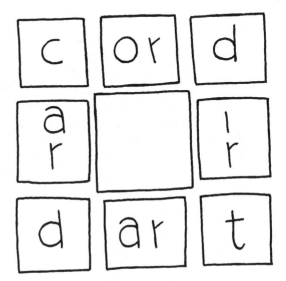

ACTIVITY TWIST

Invite the child to make up his or her own corner-to-corner puzzle and challenge you to fill it out.

PHONICS SALAD

36

Toss some phonics in your recipe for a healthy, educational salad!

WHAT YOU'LL NEED: salad ingredients, large bowl, salad spoons, salad dressing, pencil, paper

Explain to the child that there are all sorts of salads, including vegetable salad, fruit salad, and salad with meat or pasta. Begin by listing all of the ingredients you can put into a salad. Next make a real salad using only ingredients that have a short vowel sound. For example, suggest a tossed vegetable salad that could have any or all of the following short vowel ingredients: lettuce, radish, celery, mushroom, egg, asparagus, olive, ham, bell pepper, and others. Top the salad with a favorite dressing, and enjoy the finished product! (If you do not want to make a real salad, you can easily adapt this activity to writing the ingredients on a recipe card.)

LONG VOWEL HUNT

37

In the cupboard? In the toy box? Who knows where the child will find objects needed for this vowel hunt.

WHAT YOU'LL NEED: construction paper, markers

Fold a large piece of paper into five columns. Write these headings at the top: Long A, Long E, Long I, Long O, Long U. Review these sounds together. Next have the child walk around the house or yard in search of objects that contain one of the vowel sounds. Ask the child to find at least three objects for each long vowel. Have the child write the name of each object found in the appropriate column on the paper.

38

STAR MOBILE

▼▼▼▼▼▼▼▼▼▼▼▼▼▼▼▼▼▼▼▼▼▼▼▼▼▼▼▼▼▼▼

Star light, star bright, the first star the child sees tonight will be from this attractive vowel mobile.

WHAT YOU'LL NEED: sturdy paper, blunt scissors, aluminum foil, markers, masking tape, heavy string, clear tape

Cut a piece of sturdy paper into a large star shape, cover it with aluminum foil, and write the word *star* on it. Then cut out several small star shapes, covering each with aluminum foil. Next invite the child to find other examples of words with the letter pattern *ar.* Have him or her write each word on a piece of masking tape, and attach it to the smaller star shapes—one word per star. Tape pieces of heavy string to the top of each small star. Complete the mobile by taping the smaller stars to the larger one as shown.

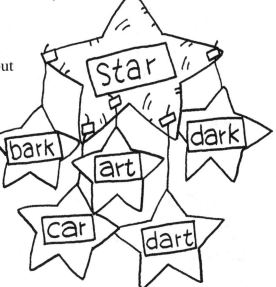

ACTIVITY TWIST

Invite the child to make other mobiles using star shapes and words that contain the following letter patterns:

bird	*ir*	horse	*or*
letter	*er*	purse	*ur*

WRITING ROUNDUPS

Learning the fundamental skills of writing can be an enjoyable and creative experience for any child. With your guidance, the following assortment of activities—from making collages and writing top ten lists to creating poems—will open up an exciting world of writing to the young learner. Even though the activities are labeled by their level of difficulty, *all* activities are on the same level of fun. Feel free to adapt and change them, using whatever resources you have available to you. Many activities can be enhanced by adding illustrations. Be creative!

39 DESCRIBE YOURSELF!

Writing down descriptive words about yourself is a fun and creative way to learn about who you are!

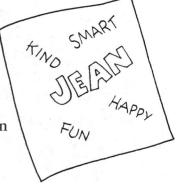

WHAT YOU'LL NEED: markers or crayons, paper, old magazines, blunt scissors, glue

Begin this activity by having the child brainstorm descriptive words about who he or she is—*smart, kind, happy, fun*. Next, help the child look for the descriptive words in old magazines and cut them out together. Have the child use a crayon or marker to write his or her name on a piece of paper. Glue the words to the paper around the name.

40 ACROSTIC POETRY

This easy form of poetry can be used whenever a special day, person, or event calls for a poem.

WHAT YOU'LL NEED: paper, markers

Perhaps it is Father's Day and the child needs to make a card. Suppose a special friend or family member needs a comforting thought. To create an acrostic poem, have the child write a key word, such as *father,* vertically on the left side of the paper. On each line, write a related word that begins with each letter, creating a poem such as the following:

Fun

Always helping

Terrific

Hardworking

Exciting

Ready

For variety, the child can use two or more words for each line, creating a series of phrases.

LOOPING INTO WRITING

41

Looping helps get the brain working and provides a fundamental process for focusing on an idea.

WHAT YOU'LL NEED: paper, pencil

Begin by inviting the child to do three minutes of freewriting, which means writing any words or phrases that come to mind. Encourage the child to write the entire time. Tell her or him not to worry about the quality of the writing, punctuation, and so on. When time is up, have the child reread the work and circle one good idea. Then encourage the child to write about that idea for two to three minutes. Again, when time is up, have the child reread the work and circle one good idea. You may need to repeat this process one more time.

When finished, the child will be ready to begin writing on the topic and be happy with the starting point. Encourage the child to use this process as a writing technique, and you'll be developing a writer!

42

JOKING AROUND

Consider "the source" when you need some laughter to liven up your day!

WHAT YOU'LL NEED: stapler, paper, joke books (optional), pencil

Staple several pieces of paper together to make a book. Have the child write jokes you have heard in the book. Go to the library, and check out some joke books. Then have the child write favorite jokes found in the joke book. The child can also try creating original jokes or revising existing jokes to add to the collection. Share with friends and family, and have a constant source of laughter.

MY BODY AND ME

*Combine art and writing while the child learns
his or her body size and parts.*

WHAT YOU'LL NEED: butcher paper, pencil, blunt scissors, sticky notes

Begin by placing a large piece of butcher paper on the floor. The paper should be big enough for the child to lie on. Then take a pencil, and trace around the child. Next have the child use scissors to cut out the outline. Have the child write names of body parts on sticky notes, then place the notes on the appropriate parts of the body.

Vary this activity by having the child lie on the paper in amusing poses; a weight lifter, for instance. Have the child draw the barbells on another piece of paper and add them to the drawing. Another variation includes adding clothes for different types of weather, such as a coat, hat, or pair of pants. Lay the clothing on the paper, following the same outlining process, and have the child label the clothing. "Dress" the body parts when planning how to get ready for a rainy, sunny, or snowy day.

VERSES AND MORE VERSES

*You don't have to be a trained singer to have fun
with this singing and writing activity.*

WHAT YOU'LL NEED: paper, pencil

Sing a favorite song together such as "Hush Little Baby," "Eensy, Weensy Spider," or "There Was an Old Woman Who Swallowed a Fly." Explain how most simple songs rhyme and discuss what a rhyme is. Show and explain how new verses are sometimes written for fun to be shared with others. Then try creating some new verses and singing them together. Have the child write the new verses on a piece of paper. Encourage the child to share with others, inviting them to add verses to the song, too.

SIMILE POEMS

45

Once the child understands similes, they become easier to create!

WHAT YOU'LL NEED: paper, pencil, examples of similes from poetry books for young children

This form of poetry is perfect for honoring a family member, creating a special card, or delighting a friend. The simile poem uses several sentences that have similes, which are two unlike thoughts that are compared to each other. The key words that identify a simile are *like* and *as*. The poem can be as short as two lines, such as the following examples, or as long as the young poet prefers. For an extension, have the child consider making a "simile book" and keeping favorites that are heard or read for use in later writings.

Mother is **like** a soft pillow.

Her lap is as soft **as** a cloud.

My cat is **like** a ball of fur.

Her paws are as soft **as** velvet.

FOOD RIDDLE

46

Describing food characteristics will enhance the child's descriptive vocabulary—and make your mouth water!

WHAT YOU'LL NEED: foods that have distinctive characteristics (orange, apple, banana, squash, and so on), paper, pencil

Have the child choose a food and make a list of all its characteristics without telling what the food is. For example, suggest that the list for an orange include words such as *bumpy, round, sweet,* and so on. Invite the child to try to stump you by reading all the characteristics of a particular food without telling its name.

47

TAKE A MESSAGE

• •

Taking a phone message is an important skill and can be taught using fairy tales.

WHAT YOU'LL NEED: fairy tales, pink message forms or notepaper, pencil

Read a favorite fairy tale, such as *Little Red Riding Hood*, aloud with the child. Discuss what Little Red might have said if she had phoned home when the wolf was about to eat her: "Mom! Call the woodsman! Grandmother is too hairy!" What message would the three bears have left with the police if Goldilocks hadn't run away? Have the child write the message on the pink pad or notepaper.

ACTIVITY TWIST

Brainstorm with the child about what Little Red's mother might have said after she received the message about Grandmother? Invite the child to write a new story ending.

SENSE-A-TIONAL POEM

This irresistible form of poetry helps budding poets understand the body's senses.

WHAT YOU'LL NEED: paper, pencil

Introduce the body's five senses: taste, hearing, smell, sight, and touch. Talk about how each of these senses helps the child appreciate the world. Think of a topic or idea that could be described by the senses, such as food, a season, or an event (carnival, birthday, holiday). Explain the format of the sample poem below. Then share the example poem. Have the child create a poem using the same format.

Winter

Line 1: color of topic or idea	Winter wears white and gray.
Line 2: tastes like	It tastes like ice on the tongue.
Line 3: sounds like	It sounds like whispers in the night,
Line 4: smells like	Yet it smells cool and clear.
Line 5: looks like	It looks like a fairyland in the dark
Line 6: feels like	And sends shivers to all who feel its chill.

FAMILY NEWSLETTER

49

Start a family tradition that benefits everyone, especially if family members live far apart.

WHAT YOU'LL NEED: pencil, paper, envelope, postage stamp

Invite the child to create a newsletter that has one or more short articles about family events. The newsletter can be as simple as one page written in pencil or as elaborate as something done on a computer, complete with special fonts and art. Then have the child send the newsletter to a relative along with a list of other relatives' addresses and the route the newsletter should take. A note asking all recipients to add their news to the newsletter should also be enclosed.

When it arrives back to the child, he or she should replace the information that has circulated with new information. Then have the child send it off again, following the same route as the first edition of the newsletter, instructing family members to replace circulated information with new information. This way everyone gets the latest family news without having to write individual letters to family members.

SLEEPY TIME RECIPE

50

Getting ready for bed can be a sweet experience with this writing and sharing activity.

WHAT YOU'LL NEED: paper, pencil

Discuss with the child the interesting things that happen at night. For example, the stars come out, the fairies put stardust in the child's eyes, and the moon comes up. Talk about recipes and how ingredients can be carefully mixed to make a special treat. Have the child make a list of all the ingredients that would be perfect for a good night's sleep. Then invite the child to create a recipe, deciding what amounts would be just right. For example, a child may want two cups of stardust to dust the whole room or maybe just a pinch for the eyes. Is the whole moon necessary or just a slice?

After the child has written the recipe, have the child read it at bedtime. For a variation, make a wake-up recipe using the same process.

51

WHERE WOULD I LIVE?

Learning how to compare features of different places can be a useful skill. Start by comparing city and country.

WHAT YOU'LL NEED: paper, pencil

Have the child make a chart by writing CITY on one side of the paper and COUNTRY on the other. Then have the child list the features of each area. Once the features have been listed, discuss the advantages and disadvantages of both areas. Follow the example on the right.

COUNTRY	CITY
Quiet	Exciting
Fields	Streets
Trees	Buildings

52

TOP TEN LISTS

Making lists is a popular and fun way to motivate a reluctant writer.

WHAT YOU'LL NEED: paper, pencil

Invite the child to create a list of his or her top ten all-time favorite things to do, such as staying in bed. Then he or she can create a list of reasons to do the opposite, such as in these examples:

TEN REASONS TO STAY IN BED	TEN REASONS TO GET OUT OF BED
It's a school day.	It's a school day.
I haven't studied for spelling.	I need to study for spelling.
My toe hurts.	Mom will tell me to wash dishes if I stay home.
My turtle will be lonely if I go.	My turtle wants to hibernate.
My friend is sick.	My friend is coming over.
It's meat loaf day at school.	It's brownie day at school.
My pinkie hurts.	Dad will tell me to clean the house if I stay home.
My dog will be lonely if I go.	My dog just wants to sleep anyway.
It's raining outside.	I can go out and see a rainbow.
I want to watch television.	Mom unplugged the television.

ACTIVITY TWIST

While the child writes one version of a top ten list, write your own amusing list of reasons why you should or should not stay in bed. Compare lists for added enjoyment.

WORD WHEEL

53

*Get rolling with wordplay in this activity,
and explore words that move.*

WHAT YOU'LL NEED: paper, pencil

Draw a wheel, using the example on the right as your guide. Be sure to include spokes and a round area in the center. Invite the child to choose something that moves, such as a bicycle, in-line skates, or wheelbarrow. Then have the child write the chosen word in the center of the wheel. Talk about all the words you can think of relating to that word. For example, a bicycle may have handlebars, brakes, a seat, gears, and so on. Have the child write the related words between the spokes as shown.

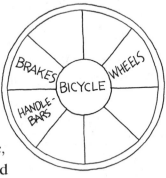

WORD COLLAGE

54

*Words take on a personality all their own when they are
artistically arranged in a collage. Get creative!*

WHAT YOU'LL NEED: magazines, blunt scissors, paper, glue or clear tape

Work with a variety of topics that contain words found in magazines. Good examples include food, fashion, sports, and music. Choose a topic. Then find related words in magazine headlines or advertisements. Look for words in different fonts, colors, and artistic treatments. Have the child cut out the words. Then invite the child to place the words on the paper and create sentences, phrases, or interesting arrangements. Add appropriate punctuation to enhance the collage. Glue or tape all the pieces in place. If there is room, the child can add related pictures.

SPELLING SPECIALS

Spelling instruction is most effective when it is integrated, or linked, with reading, language, science, social studies, math, art, or any other meaningful curriculum in which the child is interested. The activities in this chapter provide a variety of opportunities for the child to learn and apply basic spelling principles. The child will enjoy word puzzles such as Letter Tiles and Spelling Volcano and be intrigued by projects such as Break the Code and Invisible Words, all of which provide useful strategies for practicing spelling.

55 — INVISIBLE WORDS

Spies and detectives have used this clever writing trick for years—invisible ink! Here's the secret recipe!

WHAT YOU'LL NEED: saucer, lemon, cotton-tip swab, white paper, iron

Squeeze some lemon juice into a saucer. Invite the child to dip a cotton-tip swab into the lemon juice and write a sentence, or message, on white paper. Have the child use new spelling words in the sentence. Then watch. As the juice dries, it becomes virtually invisible! Next have the child give you the invisible message to see if it can be read. TOP SECRET TIP FOR ADULTS ONLY: To make the words reappear, place the message facedown on top of an old towel or rag. Iron the back of the paper with a warm iron. Share the encoded message with the child, and see how many words are spelled correctly.

PICTURE DICTIONARY

56

This dictionary provides the child with a powerful tool for alphabetizing, spelling, and learning new words.

WHAT YOU'LL NEED: several 18×6-inch strips of construction paper, clear tape, markers

Invite the child to make a picture dictionary of all new spelling words. Choose words from a school spelling list or words the child wants to learn to spell. Help the child tape 18×6-inch strips of paper end to end. Fold the strip back and forth, accordion-style, creating about three sections from each 18-inch strip. Make sure there are 26 pages. Then have the child decorate the book cover.

Next the child should write one letter of the alphabet from *Aa* to *Zz* on each page. The child can then write the spelling words on the appropriate page. You may want to help the child alphabetize the words before they are written in the picture dictionary. Finally help the child write a definition for each entry and encourage him or her to include a colorful illustration, too.

PATTERN PLAY

57

Improve the child's spelling abilities with this creative approach to analyzing spelling patterns.

WHAT YOU'LL NEED: chenille stems

List words spelled with a similar pattern, and invite the child to discover how they are alike. For example, the words *took* and *cook* have the spelling pattern *ook,* and the words *night* and *light* have the spelling pattern *ight.*

Next ask the child to form each letter in the pattern by bending and twisting chenille stems. Then make chenille stem letters to add to the pattern in order to spell new words with the same pattern. How many words can the child spell with the same spelling pattern?

58

ABC ORDER

A little word processing on the computer will add pizzazz to this ABC order activity!

WHAT YOU'LL NEED: computer with word processor

Invite the child to type words from a spelling list into the computer. Show the child how to highlight and move a word to a new location on the page. Then ask the child to put the words on the list in alphabetical order. The final product can be made to look creative by changing the type to a large, decorative font before printing.

LETTER TILES

59

In this simple game, the child creates letter tiles to build spelling words!

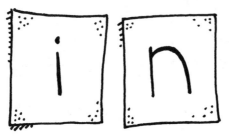

WHAT YOU'LL NEED: large index cards, markers

Help the child make three sets of letter tiles from index cards for the consonant clusters *gr, br,* and *fr.* Then make three sets of tiles for each individual letter of the alphabet, from *a* to *z.* Next invite the child to build words with the letter tiles. Encourage the child to build two words at a time, making sure that the words have at least one consonant cluster in common, as shown. Then challenge the child to build three words at a time. Continue building words until all of the consonant clusters are used up.

ACTIVITY TWIST

Once all the consonant clusters have been used up, help the child write sentences with the words made from the letter tiles.

BACKWARD BEE

▼▼▼▼▼▼▼▼▼▼▼▼▼▼▼▼▼▼▼▼▼▼▼▼▼▼▼▼▼▼▼▼▼▼▼▼ **60**

*Spelling words backward is just as fun as spelling
words forward. Try it and see!*

WHAT YOU'LL NEED: paper, pencil

Begin by providing a list of words for the child to spell. They may be words from a school spelling list or words the child wants to learn to spell. Then, just like in a regular spelling bee, give the child a word to spell. However, instead of spelling the word forward, have the child spell it backward. The child gets one point for each word spelled correctly.

61 ▬ ▬ ▬ ▬ ▬ # SPELLING VOLCANO ▬ ▬ ▬ ▬

*Engage the child in this challenging activity of
wits and vocabulary.*

WHAT YOU'LL NEED: paper, pencil

Begin by drawing boxes in the shape of a volcano, like the example shown here, but don't fill in the letters: two boxes at the top, followed by a row of three boxes, a row of four boxes, a row of five boxes, and so on to seven. Then write a two-letter word in the top row, perhaps *an*. Have the child add one new letter to the previous word to spell a new word. Write the new word on the second row of the volcano. Continue in this way, adding one new letter each time, going as far down the volcano as possible. Can the child make it to the bottom?

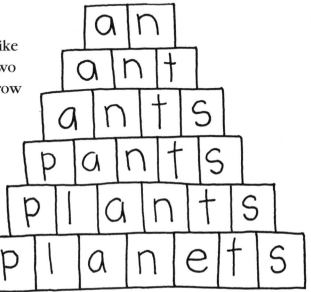

BREAK THE CODE

The child becomes a spelling sleuth while trying to break secret codes.

WHAT YOU'LL NEED: paper, felt-tip pens, blunt scissors

Help the child make a code breaker. Use a felt-tip pen to draw a wheel pattern like the one shown here. Cut out the wheel. Write the letters of the alphabet in sequential order in the spaces on the outer edge of the largest wheel and their corresponding numbers, 1–26, on the inner wheel as shown.

Next write a secret message in code on a separate piece of paper; that is, substitute the corresponding number for each letter. Then the child can take on the role of a young sleuth and decode the secret message by using the code breaker. For example, using the encoder shown, the following message says:

13-5-5-20 13-5 1-20 20-8-5
6-15-18-20!

M-E-E-T M-E A-T T-H-E F-O-R-T!

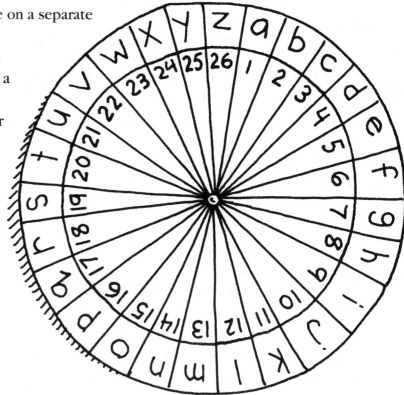

APPLE TREE

63

There is more to an apple tree when the child plays
this version of the game of hangman.

WHAT YOU'LL NEED: masking tape, paper, pencil

Before play begins, make a ladder with masking tape on a tile floor or smooth surface. Make five rungs on the ladder. Then draw an apple tree on paper. Next think of a specific spelling word, perhaps one from the child's school spelling list or a word the child may want to learn to spell. Then draw a row of apples on the tree.

Next have the child stand on the bottom rung of the ladder and try to guess one letter that is part of the word. Every correct letter gets written in the appropriate apple. For every incorrect guess, the child must step up one rung on the ladder. The game ends when the child guesses the spelling of the word correctly, or if he or she "steps off the top of the ladder." Ready to play again? Just erase the letters on the tree, and start the game over.

64

WORD SQUARE

Here's a head-scratcher that will keep the child
thinking long after it is put down.

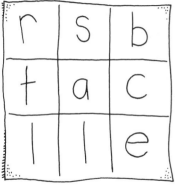

WHAT YOU'LL NEED: paper, pencil

Copy a word square like the one shown here on a piece of paper. Begin by having the child choose any letter in the puzzle and start building a word. Explain that each letter in the word being built must touch another letter in the square. To accomplish this the child can move up, down, across, or diagonally around the square. Demonstrate by spelling the word *ball*. Encourage the child to spell as many words as possible using the letters in the square.

PALINDROME PALS

65

The child will want to back up and start again with this wacky activity that puts spelling in forward motion.

Explain to the child that a palindrome is a word that is spelled the same forward or backward. Some examples are *mom* and *toot.* Invite the child to see how many palindromes he or she can come up with. Use the following clues to help the child get started: another name for father (*dad*); the sound made by a baby chick (*peep*); the sound made by a bursting balloon (*pop*); a body part for seeing (*eye*); the time in the middle of the day (*noon*).

66

MAGIC WORDS

Put a magic spell on some familiar words and turn them into new words. Just say "Abracadabra!"

Pose the following question to the child: How do you turn a cap into a cape? The answer: With magic! A magic *e*, that is. Show the child how adding an *e* to some words will "magically" turn them into other words.

Next invite the child to put a magic spell on words such as *tub* and *cub,* turning them into the new words *tube* and *cube.* Ask the child to think of other words that could fall under the same spell. You may want to suggest the following words to get the child started: *tap, her, cut, kit, rip, rob,* and *can.*

GRAMMAR GRABBERS

Taking an interactive approach to developing grammar, this chapter is jam-packed with creative, fun, hands-on projects that integrate spelling, usage, and vocabulary. The child will learn about nouns, verbs, pronouns, adjectives, and all the other essential grammar elements by getting involved in activities such as Yak-a-Sak!, making a poster in Lost and Found, and much more. Sound like fun? It is! So get ready for a grammar extravaganza.

67 TEN QUESTIONS

While enjoying this game of questions and answers,
the child will develop sentence sense.

WHAT YOU'LL NEED: small objects, bag or box, notebook paper, pencil

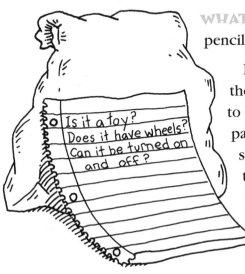

Place an object, such as a hairbrush, inside a bag or box. Invite the child to ask questions about the object in the bag in an effort to discover its identity. Write the questions on a piece of notebook paper, pointing out the capital letter at the beginning of each sentence and the question mark at the end, before answering them. A maximum of ten questions can be asked before the object is revealed; however, at any time during the question and answer exchange, the child can try to guess the object. If the child correctly identifies the object, a new object is placed in the bag and play is continued.

68 LOST AND FOUND

*Where, oh, where, has my favorite
storybook character gone?*

WHAT YOU'LL NEED: favorite storybooks, construction paper, crayons or markers

LOST!
Troll

He is gruff and grumpy.
He has a long nose with a wart on it.
If you see him, call the Bridge Keeper.

Place a few favorite storybooks in a quiet reading area and provide ample time for the child to browse through the books before you begin.

Begin by inviting the child to make a lost and found poster for a storybook character. Encourage the child to describe the lost character. Explain that the reader will want to know who is lost, what the character looks like, and anything else that would help with identification. Allow the child to return to the book area, if needed, to look for pictures of the selected character or to double-check information.

As the child works on the poster, have him or her include information as to what should be done if the lost character is found. Encourage creative thinking and spontaneity as the child creates the poster.

NAMES, NAMES, NAMES 69

*Get out your markers, and write up a stack of labels
for items around the house.*

WHAT YOU'LL NEED: 3×5-inch index cards, stickers, or sentence strips; markers; dictionary

Set out index cards, stickers, or sentence strips and a box of markers. Invite the child to make labels for objects (nouns) in the house, such as furniture, a computer, items on a desk, and so on. Encourage the child to use a dictionary for the correct spelling of each noun before writing it. Then have the child display the labels beside the objects.

70 GET IN THE ACTION

*A beloved Mother Goose rhyme becomes
a foundation for teaching verbs.*

Sing a few verses of "Here We Go 'Round the Mulberry Bush" with the child. Invite the child to pantomime the actions. Explain that a word describing action is called a *verb*. Then have the child create his or her own verse, following the examples below. Ask the child what verb(s) he or she pantomimed in the verse.

Here we go 'round the mulberry bush,
the mulberry bush, the mulberry bush.
Here we go 'round the mulberry bush,
So early in the morning.

Verse 2. This is the way we wash our hands.
Verse 3. This is the way we wash our clothes.
Verse 4. This is the way we go to school.
Verse 5. (Make up a verse.)

PAST TENSE SENSE 71

*The child will identify and use past tense verbs
while creating a decorative scrapbook page.*

WHAT YOU'LL NEED: scrapbook page (or heavy paper), photo (or drawing) of the child, clear tape or glue, decorating supplies

Help the child make a scrapbook page. Begin by having the child tape the picture or drawing on the page. Encourage the child to decorate the page using one or more of the following suggestions: paint a border, glue or tape a paper frame around the picture, use fancy letters to write a caption, add ticket stubs or other souvenirs associated with the picture. Invite the child to write a sentence at the bottom of the scrapbook page to tell what happened. Remind him or her to write in the past tense.

YAK-A-SAK!

72

Forming sentences by combining random sentence parts is a hilarious way to practice building sentences.

WHAT YOU'LL NEED: pencil, sentence strips, 2 sacks

Begin by writing sentence parts on sentence strips. Make up five to six simple subjects, or naming parts. An example of a subject is *red, juicy tomatoes.* Write five to six simple predicates, or telling parts. An example of a predicate is *are growing in the garden.* Place the two sentence parts in separate sacks. Next have the child pick one sentence part from each sack and combine them to make a sentence. Prepare yourself for some silly sentences.

ACTIVITY TWIST

For additonal creative fun, invite the child to illustrate the silly sentences with pencils or crayons.

LISTENING LAUNCHES

Listening involves the ability to hear and distinguish sounds in words, a skill necessary when translating written symbols into sounds and words, which is the foundation of reading. Through listening, the child will not only develop these abilities but will build vocabulary skills and learn the building blocks of verbal communication. Included in this chapter are a wide variety of activities that offer the child an opportunity to develop good listening skills and to have fun engaging in challenging activities at the same time.

73 — WHAT'S THE LETTER?

This guessing game is a simple phonics activity that can be done anytime and anywhere. It's great for traveling.

Begin by pointing to an object in the room or a picture in a magazine or book. Say the name of the object (person, animal, tree, flower, etc.). Ask the child to name the beginning letter. Continue to offer new items for letter guessing, or invite the child to choose an object and give you a turn at guessing.

To increase the difficulty of the game, offer a two- or three-word description of the object and ask the child to say the first letter of the object. The more unusual the items chosen for the game, the more interesting the game can be!

74

RHYME-A-STORY

By listening for rhymes, the child will practice comprehension while creating a story.

Make up a story together but tell it in rhymes. Begin by making up the first sentence. For example, you might say, "The dog went for a walk." Invite the child to make up a rhyming sentence, then another sentence for you to rhyme. Explain to the child that his or her second sentence does not have to rhyme with his or her first sentence. For example, the child would add "The dog began to talk. Then the dog began to run." Then you would continue with: "He wanted to get out of the sun. He found a tree to lie under." Continue until you and the child are satisfied with the ending.

DO YOU REMEMBER?

75

Sharing facts with the child is an interesting exercise to enhance listening and strengthen memory.

Begin by telling ten things about yourself to the child. Your list may include such things as "I like dogs," "yesterday I ate spaghetti for dinner," or "the red shirt I am wearing is the one Grandma gave me." Then invite the child to tell ten personal facts as well.

After both of you have recited a list of ten personal facts, take turns trying to remember and repeat as many of the statements from the other person's list as possible.

SECRET WORD

76

*Listening for verbal clues helps determine the
meaning of unknown words.*

Choose a word, and keep it a secret. It must be a word that is used often, such as *water* or a pet's name. Then agree on a sound for the secret word together—for example, tapping your foot or whistling. Each time the word comes up in conversation, you will perform the signal. The game can take place during other activities such as preparing lunch, cleaning the house, or taking a walk. How long does it take the child to determine what the secret word is?

77

WHAT WAS THAT SOUND?

*This simple game enhances the child's listening
skills and can be played anytime.*

Have the child close his or her eyes and listen carefully. Then make a sound by using a common household item: shake a key chain, switch a light off and on, open and close a drawer, or rapidly flip through the pages of a book. After you have made the sound, ask the child to guess the name of the object making the sound.

STORY OPPOSITES

78

Invite the child to demonstrate good listening skills by turning a story into its opposite.

Take turns creating opposite versions of the same story. Begin by telling a simple story. Ask the child to retell the story, changing as many things as possible to their opposites. You may want to offer suggestions to get the child started. In the story *Cinderella,* for example, you might tell of how the shoe did *not* fit. After the child has taken a turn, discuss any other opposites that could be added to the story. Then invite the child to make up or read a story for you to change, or give the child another attempt at a new story.

79

SOUND SWITCH

Changing one word a little at a time is a fun way to learn how to analyze the parts and sounds of words.

Explain to the child that you both will take turns changing a word, one sound at a time. Then choose a word that has two or more syllables. Take the first turn, and change one sound. Then invite the child to try to change another sound in the word. Continue to change the word, sound by sound, until you are both satisfied that the word is quite different than the original. Use the following example to get you started.

EXAMPLE: bubble, rubble, ripple, triple, triplet, tripping, sipping, skipping, skipper

SPEAKING SPARKS

Writers use language to communicate meaning. Readers, in turn, use language to discern meaning. The more experiences the child has with language in all its forms, the more success he or she is likely to experience at the pleasurable task of reading. Language is an active process, which is learned through use. The child will learn and internalize vocabulary, sentence structure, and meaning through the use of words, sentences, and sounds, all of which express ideas and emotions. Here is a wide variety of language activities to enjoy with the child that provide different ways to experiment with and experience speaking.

80 STORY FLIPS

These story-building squares offer the child infinite imaginative possibilities.

WHAT YOU'LL NEED: paper, crayons or markers, old magazines, blunt scissors, 8×10-inch cardboard squares, clear tape or glue

Build stories by flipping pictures the child has drawn or cut out of old magazines. The pictures should include animals, people, and objects. Help the child glue or tape each picture onto its own cardboard square. Once you and the child have assembled 12 to 20 pictures, ask the child to sort them into four random piles. Invite the child to turn over a square from each pile and then make up a story based on the four pictures. Continue with another set of four pictures for endless creative story-building fun!

The woman went shopping to buy a dog to give to her cat.

THIRD-PERSON TALES

81

This activity stretches the child's ability to relay experiences from a new perspective.

Invite the child to tell you about an event in his or her day. Explain that you want the child to tell it to you in the third person—in other words, the child should tell about an event that happened during the day as if it happened to someone else.

For example, instead of saying "I got up early today," the child would begin by saying "He (or she) got up early today."

82

NEWS REPORT INTERVIEWS

Get the "scoop" while practicing research and organizational skills.

WHAT YOU'LL NEED: paper, pencil

Invite the child to be a news reporter and report on an event that happened at home or while on a family outing. Choose a topic together for the interview. It may be something as ordinary as dinner last night or a little more unusual, such as what happened when the dog got out. Encourage the child to ask you questions that will uncover as many details as possible. He or she should write down the answers on a piece of paper. Then invite the child to give a news report as if reporting the story on the evening news.

DON'T SAY WHAT YOU SEE!

83

This picture description activity challenges the child to find the right words to convey meaning.

WHAT YOU'LL NEED: 3×5-inch index cards, markers, old magazines, blunt scissors, clear tape or glue, shoe box

Create 15 to 20 picture cards of common animals or objects together. The cards can be simple line drawings on index cards or pictures cut from old magazines and glued or taped onto index cards. Put the cards in the shoe box.

Then invite the child to pull out a card and describe what is pictured without naming the object. Make sure the child keeps the card hidden from your view. You are now allowed five guesses to determine what is on the card. After the answer has been guessed or given, it is your turn to pick a card, describe what is pictured, and ask the child to guess its identity.

84

WORD EMPHASIS

Change the meaning of a sentence by emphasizing a different word.

Discuss the different ways of conveying meaning when using the same sentence. Make up a simple sentence, and have the child repeat the sentence, emphasizing a different word each time. The sentence can be as simple as, "The pretty cat sleeps all day." Talk about how the meaning of the sentence changed each time a different word was emphasized.

PROVE IT!

● **85**

*Challenge the child to use critical thinking
skills to "show what you know."*

Make a statement, and ask the child to think about the statement and then guess whether the statement is true or false. After the child has answered, ask why the answer was chosen. How did the child decide or know that your statement was true or false? How can the child prove that the statement was either true or false? Encourage the child to back up his or her statement.

86

MAKE IT MODERN

▼▼▼▼▼▼▼▼▼▼▼▼▼▼▼▼▼▼▼▼▼▼▼▼

*In this creative retelling activity, the child brings
favorite characters to life in modern times.*

Invite the child to retell a familiar folk or fairy tale, such as *The Three Little Pigs* or *Cinderella,* but change the setting to modern times and to the place where you live. If the story took place today, what would be the same? What would be different? If the three little pigs were building their house next door, what materials would they use? Whom would they ask for supplies? If Cinderella lived in your town, where would she live? Where would the prince live? What would she wear to the ball?

CHARACTER INTERVIEW

87

Encourage the child to interpret information and make predictions while pretending to be a favorite character.

Invite the child to pretend to be a character from a favorite story. Explain that you are going to interview the character, and the child should answer all your questions as the character would. Ask questions that wouldn't necessarily be found in the original story. For example, ask the character about favorite foods, what kind of stories the character likes to read, what the character wants to be when it grows up.

After you interview the child/character, choose another character together and switch roles. Now it's the child's turn to interview you!

88 ELABORATE, EXAGGERATE

The child will delight in this exaggeration game that cultivates descriptive language skills.

Begin by making a simple statement, and invite the child to add some exaggerations to it. Explain that when one exaggerates, a lot of descriptive language, real or unreal, is added. For example, if you say "The bear went to the store," the child might reply "The big bear went to the honey store." After the child adds some descriptive words, take a turn yourself and exaggerate the statement further. Continue taking turns until the original statement has become an elaborate, descriptive sentence that can be either funny or serious.

89 AS THE STORY TURNS

This is an enjoyable way for the child to practice summarizing information and sequencing skills.

Retell a favorite and familiar story with the child, one event at a time. Invite the child to begin the story by retelling the first event in his or her own words. Then take your turn and tell the next event. Continue taking turns until the story is finished.

TELL IT BACKWARD! 90

Here's a twist on storytelling—start with the ending first!

This challenging backward storytelling activity helps develop sequence understanding, comprehension, and story recall. Take turns retelling a favorite story with the child, only tell the story in reverse. You might want to have the book handy while retelling.

Begin telling at the end of the story. Then invite the child to tell the part that happened just before the ending. Take another turn, and tell what happened before that. Continue taking turns until the whole story has been told, event by event, from end to beginning.

USING BRAINPOWER

Good readers are problem solvers. They use critical thinking skills to process the words they read. They construct meaning while they read by interpreting information, making predictions, and hypothesizing. Good readers bring a sense of curiosity to what they read. They are detectives searching for significance. They reflect on the words they process and draw conclusions based on their own prior knowledge. Good readers think while they read. Problem solving is a skill, and like any skill, it takes practice. Here is an assortment of activities to challenge the child and help develop thinking skills.

91 WHAT IF?

This game fosters imaginative thinking while the child responds to "what if" situations.

Make up an interesting "what if" situation, and invite the child to act out a response. The following are some suggestions:

What if a bird flew in the window and started playing with your toys?

What if it started raining in your house?

What if you ate a hamburger that tasted like pizza?

Have the child dramatize or explain what actions might be taken *if* a particular event occurred. How would the child react to each situation?

92 THE SAME & DIFFERENT

Play this game to develop the child's abilities to perceive relationships and make comparisons.

Name any two items, and invite the child to tell one way in which the items are similar and one way in which they are different. Begin with easy comparisons, such as a cat and a dog, and increase the difficulty as you go along. Answers for easy comparisons will be more obvious while the more difficult comparisons will require some creative thinking.

The child might suggest a dog and cat are similar because they both are animals, but different because one meows and the other barks. For a comparison of a star and a television, the child might suggest they both glow or you can look at both of them, but one is close and the other is far away.

Accept all answers that make good connections, and encourage the child to be creative in his or her responses.

REVEALING SENTENCES 93

Exercise creative and critical thinking while using one word as an anchor to create an entire sentence.

WHAT YOU'LL NEED: pencil, paper

Choose a word that represents a person, place, or thing. The word should be plural unless it is someone's name. Invite the child to make a sentence using the letters of the word to determine the first letter of each word in the sentence. The chosen word should be the first word of the sentence.

For example, if the word chosen was *cars,* the sentence could be: **C**ars **A**re **R**eally **S**uper. A sentence for *cats* might be: **C**ats **A**re **T**imid **S**ometimes. A sentence for *Jim* might be: **J**im **I**s **M**essy.

CARS ARE REALLY SUPER

94

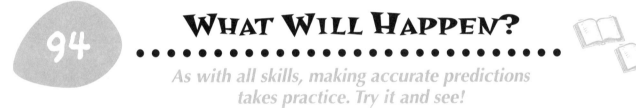

WHAT WILL HAPPEN?

*As with all skills, making accurate predictions
takes practice. Try it and see!*

WHAT YOU'LL NEED: paper, pencil

Before you and the child go on an errand, shopping, or out visiting, discuss what you might see and hear and what might happen. Make a list of predictions. After returning from your trip, check the list and see how many of the predictions were accurate.

GOOD NEWS, BAD NEWS

95

*Good news, bad news stories are fun to create
and often produce a lot of laughter.*

Create a good news, bad news story together. Each person takes a turn telling something good that happened followed by something bad. The next person must continue the story by adding the next good thing followed by the next bad thing.

For example, the first person might start by saying, "I found a magic stone in the park. That was good. I lost it on the way home. That was bad." The second person might then continue with, "My friend found my stone. That was good. He wouldn't give it back. That was bad."

MEMORY MADNESS

96

Here's a simple activity that helps sharpen the child's ability to remember details.

Invite the child to remember as many details as possible about a recent adventure, visit, or even a walk around the block. Then ask the child questions that challenge his or her memory skills.

What did the child hear, see, taste, smell, or touch? What was the weather like? Were there birds in the sky? Was a radio playing? What song was playing? Were people standing with their feet together or apart? Which hand petted the cat? This can be an ongoing activity for you to do periodically with the child.

97

I'M THINKING OF...

Making these simple observation puzzles helps the child practice describing what he or she sees.

Invite the child to describe a plant, animal, object, or person that can be seen in a room without mentioning its name or what it is. See if you can guess what the child is describing. After the answer has been given, describe something you see in the room and invite the child to guess. To increase the difficulty of the game, include any plant, animal, object, or person that is not in the room.

HINKIE-PINKIE

98

This activity challenges the child to use critical thinking, rhyming skill, and cleverness!

A "hinkie-pinkie" is a riddle in which the answer is a two-word rhyme. If the rhyming words have one syllable, the riddle is a "hink-pink." If the words have two syllables it is a "hinkie-pinkie."

Begin by telling the child whether the riddle is a hink-pink or a hinkie-pinkie, then present the riddle. Here are two examples:

Hink-Pink: What is a chubby pet that meows? (fat cat)

Hinkie-Pinkie: What is a puppy that got all soaking wet in the rain? (soggy doggy)

99

PEEKABOO PICTURES

This observation activity will encourage the child to see "the big picture!"

WHAT YOU'LL NEED: old magazine, blunt scissors, paper, clear tape or glue

Create peekaboo pictures by cutting a picture from an old magazine and gluing or taping it onto a sheet of paper. Do not let the child see the picture. Next cut a small circle or square in a second piece of paper. This will be the guessing page. Then take the guessing page, and lay it on top of the picture. The small portion of the picture viewed through the peekaboo hole becomes the clue for the child to guess the identity of the bigger picture. Repeat with several pictures.

SEQUENCE SENTENCES

This game helps the child recognize sequence and organize information.

WHAT YOU'LL NEED: paper strips, pencil or marker

Make up a short story or tell of a daily event using just eight to ten sentences. Write each sentence on an individual sentence strip. Mix up the strips. Then ask the child to read the strips and determine the correct sequence of the story and order the strips accordingly.

WHAT'S THE STORY?

101

This inventive game involves creative thinking, summarizing, and problem-solving skills.

WHAT YOU'LL NEED: pictures from books or magazines

Begin by looking at a picture in a book or magazine together, and discuss what you see. Pretend that one picture illustrates an entire story. Invite the child to tell you what he or she thinks the story might be about. Discuss possible details of the story. Then have the child invent a title that would fit the story.